J
636.1
Mor   Morris, Dean
       Horses

DATE DUE		
JN 23 1983	SE 18 '85	DE 14 '89
JUN. 29 1983	AP 1 5 '87	OC 10 '90
AUG. 0 4 1983	JE 1 7 '87	JY 16 '91
AUG. 1 2 1983	JY 2 9 '87	DE 1 7 '92
SEP. 1 6 1983	AG 26 '87	MY 3 '93
OCT. 0 3 1983	SE 10 '87	APR 27 '94
FEB. 6 1984	OC 28 '87	JUL 23 '96
MAY 07 1984	MY 0 9 '88	NOV 28 '96
AUG. 7 1984	DE 6 '88	DEC 1 8 '96
AUG 25 1984	JY 20 '89	JUL 29 '97
OCT. 26 1984	OC 23 '89	AUG 1 8 '97
DEC. 1 9 1984	AG 0 4 '89	NOV 24 '97
		JUL 07 '98
		OCT 13 '98

EAU CLAIRE DISTRICT LIBRARY

MEDIALOG
Alexandria, Ky 41001

W9-AKD-928

Horses

Words by Dean Morris

80761

Raintree Childrens Books
Milwaukee • Toronto • Melbourne • London

EAU CLAIRE DISTRICT LIBRARY

Copyright © 1977, Macdonald-Raintree, Inc.

All rights reserved. No part of this book may be reproduced
or utilized in any form or by any means, electronic or mechanical,
including photocopying, recording, or by any information storage
and retrieval system, without permission in writing from the
Publisher. Inquiries should be addressed to Raintree Childrens Books,
a division of Macdonald-Raintree, Inc., 205 West Highland Avenue,
Milwaukee, Wisconsin 53203.

Library of Congress Number: 77-8243

2 3 4 5 6 7 8 9 0 81 80 79 78

Printed and bound in the United States of America.

Library of Congress Cataloging in Publication Data

Morris, Dean.
  Horses.

  (Read about)
  Includes index.
  SUMMARY: Discusses the history and training of
horses and other members of their family as
domesticated animals.
    1. Horses — Juvenile literature. 2. Equidae—
Juvenile literature. [1. Horses. 2. Equidae]
I. Title.
SF302.M67   636.1   77-8243
ISBN 0-8393-0008-5 lib. bdg.

This book has been reviewed
for accuracy by

Dr. Carol B. Stein
Curator, Museum of Zoology
The Ohio State University

Horses

The horse family has lived on earth for a long time. The first kind of horse was called *Eohippus*. It was very small. Horses slowly changed and grew larger. The changes took millions of years. *Eohippus* had toes. Later horses developed hooves.

Eohippus   **Mesohippus**   **Merychippus**

Pliohippus   horse (**Equus**)

Some of the first people lived in caves.
They painted pictures of horses on the walls
of their caves. We can visit these caves
and see the pictures. The horses look
very much like horses we see today.

Later people tamed horses. They used the horses in many ways. Farmers used them to pull plows. The plows dug up the earth to make it better for farming. Some horses are very strong. They can pull heavy loads.

Before there were cars, people often rode in carriages. They used horses to pull them. In winter people rode over the snow in sleighs. Horses pulled the sleighs too. Horses were also used to pull wagons loaded with goods.

People rode on horseback. Long ago
knights rode horses into battle. The horses
wore heavy padding. They were trained
to rear up so their riders could fight.

Soldiers who ride horses are called cavalry. A cavalry charge is a way of attacking. All the horses line up and run at the same time. The cavalry soldiers ride the horses through the enemy lines and try to kill the soldiers on the other side.

Horses were important in America's history. The Indians who lived on the plains rode small horses.

Pioneers used big, strong horses to pull their covered wagons.

In the Old West, almost everyone had a horse. Cowboys used their horses to herd cattle. They also rode horses in rodeo contests. This is still a popular sport today.

Men in the United States Cavalry protected the settlers. They were police on horseback.

a cowboy riding a rodeo horse

United States Cavalryman

The Pony Express was the mail service. Men rode their horses very fast. Horses had to be changed often. Letters were carried from place to place across the country this way.

Horses have fewer jobs today. Machines do much of the work horses used to do. But horses still help people in many ways.

Some police in Canada still use horses. These police are called Mounties. They need horses in rough country where there are few roads.

EAU CLAIRE DISTRICT LIBRARY

Today most horses are used for sports. Horse racing is exciting. Many people come to watch Thoroughbred racing.

Each horse has a box at the starting line. The horses line up. Then the gates that hold the horses in their boxes are opened, and the horses race off.

starting gates

A post beside the track marks the end
of the race. The first horse to pass the
post wins.

Sometimes the race is close. A camera
at the post takes a picture of the end of
the race. The picture shows which horse won.

finishing post

Not all horse races are on a flat track.
In some races, the horses must go over
jumps. The water jump is very hard.

A horse must be trained to jump.
Training takes a long time.

water jump

Another sport is called show jumping.
The rider rides the horse around a course.
The course has many jumps. The horse
must not knock over any of the jumps.

rustic spread jump

Many people enter their horses in contests at fairs and horse shows. Both the riders and the horses practice a long time. Each rider wants his horse to win a ribbon. Ribbons are the prizes given to the ones that do the best in each contest.

These are polo ponies. Polo is a game played by teams on horseback. Polo ponies must run fast and change direction suddenly. The riders use long-handled mallets. They try to drive a ball toward a goal as they gallop by.

Groups of people enjoy trail riding.
Their horses are strong and sure-footed.
They walk carefully in rough places.
They can go up and down mountains. Trail
riding is a good way to get to places cars
cannot go.

Special names are used for different parts of a horse's body. The parts are called points.

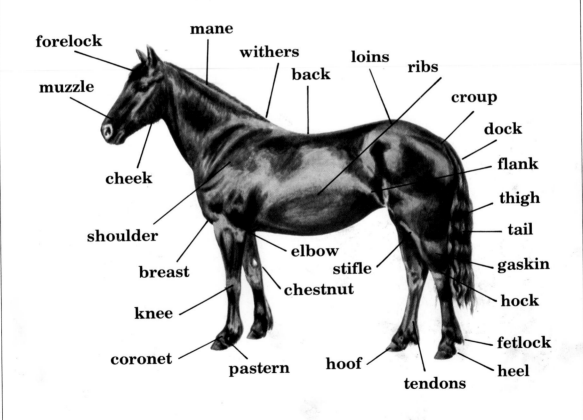

forelock

mane

withers

back

loins

ribs

croup

muzzle

dock

flank

cheek

thigh

tail

shoulder

gaskin

breast

elbow

stifle

hock

chestnut

knee

coronet

pastern

hoof

tendons

fetlock

heel

The colors of horses' coats have special names. Some horses have coats with more than one color. These mixed colors also have names. Piebald and skewbald horses are usually called pintos.

chestnut

grey

palomino

dun

piebald

Appaloosa

skewbald

strawberry roan

Arabian

Some horses are bred to be fast. Arabian horses are not very heavy. They can run very fast.

Thoroughbred horses are fast too. Fast, light horses are good for racing.

Thoroughbred

Other horses are unusually large or strong. Knights in olden times rode great horses, or Percherons. They are the largest horses.

Percheron

Shire

Other large horses are used for farm work. They are strong and can pull heavy loads.

Some horses are small.
They are called ponies.

This kind of pony is
good at climbing. It is
called a Welsh pony. It
comes from the mountain
area of Wales.

Welsh pony

Russ pony

This pony comes from
Norway. Norway is a cold
country. The pony has a
thick coat.

Shetland ponies are
very small. Only children
can ride them.

Shetland pony

It is a lot of work to take care of a
horse. Most horses have stables to live
in. The stables must be kept clean. Horses
need fresh water to drink and hay, oats,
and bran to eat.

When horses are kept outside,
they eat grass.

Several tools are needed to keep horses clean and groomed.

hoof pick

A hoof pick gets stones out of a horse's hooves.

dandy brush   body brush

curry comb

Brushes keep coats clean and shiny.

A curry comb grooms the horse's coat.

mane comb

The mane comb takes the tangles out of the mane and tail.

A rider sits in a saddle on the horse's back. Stirrups are fastened to the saddle. The rider's feet fit in the stirrups.

The bridle goes around the horse's head. It has reins to guide the horse.

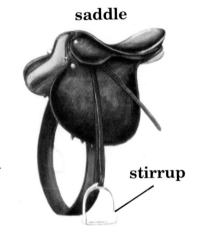

saddle

stirrup

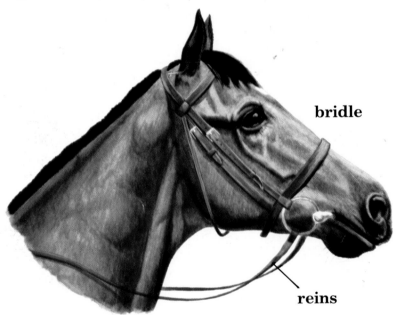

bridle

reins

Horses wear metal shoes to protect
their hooves. A person called a blacksmith
makes the U-shaped pieces of metal. He
bends each shoe to fit the hoof. Then
the shoe is nailed onto the hoof. This
does not hurt the horse.

Baby horses are called foals. Their mothers are called mares. Young foals drink their mothers' milk.

Foals learn to walk in a very short time. When they are born their legs are nearly as long as they will ever be. At first the foals follow their mothers everywhere.

Most horses are tame. Wild horses are found in only a few places. These horses live on an island in France. They live in groups called herds.

These wild ponies live in Russia. They live in herds too. Today laws protect some wild horses and ponies.

A Horse in Motion

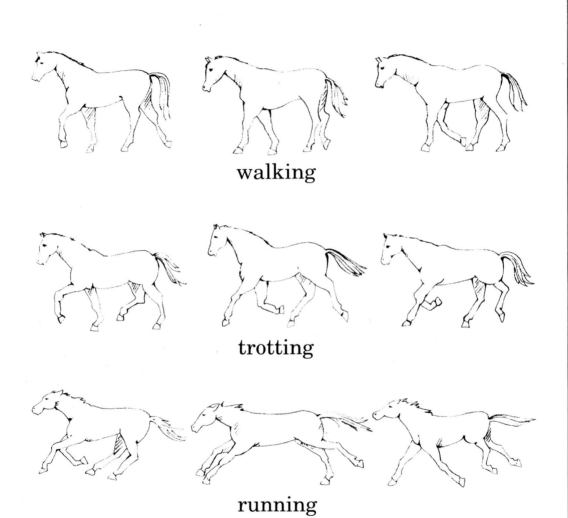

walking

trotting

running

The Skeleton of a
Domestic Horse

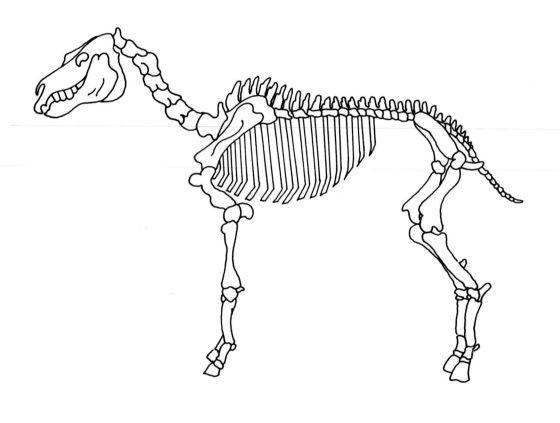

Where to Read About the Horses

race horse (rās   hôrs) *pp. 14-16, 23*
Russ pony (rus   pō′ nē) *p. 25*
Shetland pony (shet′ lənd   pō′ nē) *p. 25*
Shire (shī′ ər) *p. 24*
skewbald (skyoo′ bôld′) *p. 22*
strawberry roan (strô′ ber′ ē   rōn) *p. 22*
Thoroughbred (thur′ ō bred′) *p. 23*
Welsh pony (welsh   pō′ nē) *p. 25*

Pronunciation Key for Glossary

a	a as in **cat**, **bad**
ā	a as in **able**, ai as in **train**, ay as in **play**
ä	a as in **father**, **car**
e	e as in **bend**, **yet**
ē	e as in **me**, ee as in **feel**, ea as in **beat**, ie as in **piece**, y as in **heavy**
i	i as in **in**, **pig**
ī	i as in **ice**, **time**, ie as in **tie**, y as in **my**
o	o as in **top**
ō	o as in **old**, oa as in **goat**, ow as in **slow**, oe as in **toe**
ô	o as in **cloth**, au as in **caught**, aw as in **paw**, a as in **all**
oo	oo as in **good**, u as in **put**
o͞o	oo as in **tool**, ue as in **blue**
oi	oi as in **oil**, oy as in **toy**
ou	ou as in **out**, ow as in **plow**
u	u as in **up**, **gun**, o as in **other**
ur	ur as in **fur**, er as in **person**, ir as in **bird**, or as in **work**
yo͞o	u as in **use**, ew as in **few**
ə	a as in **again**, e as in **broken**, i as in **pencil**, o as in **attention**, u as in **surprise**
ch	ch as in **such**
ng	ng as in **sing**
sh	sh as in **shell**, **wish**
th	th as in **three**, **bath**
t̲h̲	th as in **that**, **together**

GLOSSARY

These words are defined the way they are used in this book.

another (ə nu<u>th</u>′ ər) one more

area (er′ ē ə) a certain place or part of the world

attack (ə tak′) to begin to fight against an enemy

battle (bat′ əl) a fight, usually between groups of soldiers

blacksmith (blak′ smith′) a person who uses special tools to make things out of iron, like horseshoes

body (bod′ ē) the whole of an animal or plant

bran (bran) the outer part of wheat and other grains

bred (bred) raised; mated to have young animals

bridle (brī′ dəl) headgear used to guide a horse

camera (kam′ ər ə *or* kam′ rə) a device used for taking photographs

cannot (kan′ ot *or* ka not′) is not able; can not

carriage (ker′ ij) a vehicle with wheels pulled by a horse

cavalry (kav′ əl rē) soldiers mounted on horses

cave (kāv) a natural hollow place in the ground or in the side of a mountain

charge (chärj) to attack with a rush

comb (kōm) a tool with plastic, metal, or wooden teeth, used to smooth hairs or threads

contest (kon′ test) a race or game in which each person tries to win

covered (kuv′ ərd) having a top

cowboy (kou′ boi′) a person who takes care of ranch animals

curry (kər′ ē) to groom a horse's coat

develop (di vel′ əp) to grow and change in a natural way

dug (dug) turned over soil or made a hole by digging

enjoy (en joi′) to be happy doing something

everyone (ev′ rē wun′) all the people

everywhere (ev′ rē hwer′) in all the places

fasten (fas′ ən) to put things together in a way that they cannot easily come apart

fit (fit) to be the right size

foal (fōl) a young horse

gallop (gal′ əp) to run very fast

goal (gōl) a place in a game that players try to reach in order to win a point

groom (groom) to clean, brush, and take care of a horse

guide (gīd) to show the way

hay (hā) grass that is cut and dried and used to feed animals

herd (hurd) to lead a group of several animals in a certain direction; a group of animals

history (his′ tər ē) the record of what happened before the present time

hoof (hoof *or* hŏŏf) the hard covering on the feet of such animals as horses, deer, and cattle *plural* **hooves**

hooves (hoovz) see **hoof**

horseback (hôrs′ bak′) sitting on a horse's back, riding on a horse

knight (nīt) a soldier in the Middle Ages

law (lô) a rule that must be followed by all the people in the place where the law was passed

mallet (mal′ it) a tool with a wooden head on a long pole, used in polo to hit the ball

mane (mān) long, thick hair that grows on a horse's neck

mare (mer) a female horse

metal (met′ əl) a shiny kind of material that can be melted and made into shapes for tools and other things that need to be strong

million (mil′ yən) the number 1,000,000

mix (miks) to put some different things together

nail (nāl) to drive pointed pieces of metal into something in order to fasten it

oat (ōt) a grain that comes from a grasslike plant, used to feed animals

olden (ōld′ ən) a long time ago

onto (ôn′ too *or* on′ too) to a place
on top or above

padding (pad′ ing) a thick, soft covering
used to protect something

pinto (pin′ tō) a horse or pony with a
spotted coat that has more than one color

pioneer (pī′ ə nēr′) one of the first people
to go into a new place and try to make
a home there

plain (plān) open land that is flat or
almost flat

police (pə lēs′) the persons who protect
people and see that they follow the laws
of a city or town

popular (pop′ yə lər) pleasing to many
people; liked by many people

post (pōst) a piece of wood or metal that
is made to stand up straight, used to mark
a certain point in a contest or race

rear (rēr) to get up on the back legs

rein (rān) a narrow strap used to guide a
horse

ribbon (rib′ ən) a colored piece of cloth
  that is given to the winner of a contest
rider (rī′ dər) a person who rides
rodeo (rō′ dē ō *or* rō dā′ ō) a show in
  which cowboys try to win at riding horses,
  roping calves, and other such contests
rough (ruf) not smooth or level; having
  bumps
saddle (sad′ əl) a seat for a rider put on a
  horse's back
service (sur′ vis) doing something that
  is needed by many people, such as
  moving the mail
settler (set′ lər) a person who is one of
  the first to make a home in a new place
sleigh (slā) a carriage that rests on
  runners and is pulled over snow by horses
soldier (sōl′ jər) a person who is part of
  a group that has been trained to fight
  in battles
sport (spôrt) a game or activity people
  enjoy; a contest in which people try to win

stable (stā′ bəl) a building in which
animals are kept

stirrup (stur′ əp) one of a pair of loops
that hold a rider's feet on either side
of a saddle

tame (tām) to make a wild animal learn
to be gentle and follow directions

tangles (tang′ gəlz) something twisted
together in a way that makes it hard
to be straightened out

tool (tool) something a person uses to do
work or to make something

trail (trāl) a path that is made in a
place where there are no roads and where
people do not live

unusually (un yoo′ zhoo əl ē) not happening
often; in a different way

won (wun) did better than any others
in a race or contest

Bibliography

Anderson, Clarence W. *C. W. Anderson's Complete Book of Horses and Horsemanship*. Riverside, N. J.: Macmillan Publishing Company, 1963.

Balch, Glenn. *The Book of Horses*. Englewood Cliffs, N.J.: Four Winds Press, 1967.

Berry, Barbara. *The Thoroughbreds*. Indianapolis: Bobbs-Merrill Company, 1974.

Brady, Irene. *America's Horses and Ponies*. New York: Houghton Mifflin Company, 1976.

Burton, Maurice, and Burton, Robert, editors. *The International Wildlife Encyclopedia*. 20 vols. Milwaukee: Purnell Reference Books, 1970.

Crowell, Ann. *Dawn Horse to Derby Winner: The Evolution of the Horse*. New York: Praeger, 1973.
Traces the evolution and development of the modern horse and his relatives, including the zebra, ass, mule, quagga, and tarpans.

Richards, Jane. *A Horse Grows Up*. New York: Walker & Company, 1972.
Photographs and brief text follow the development of a newly born foal as it learns to stand, walk, and explore.

Roever, J.M., and Roever, Wilfried. *The Mustangs*. Austin: Steck-Vaughn Company, 1971.
Describes the history, physical characteristics, and habits of mustangs, the wild horses that once roamed the Western grasslands.

Savitt, Sam. *True Horse Stories*. New York: Dodd, Mead & Company, 1970.
Sixteen true stories about horses from various eras and countries.

Wilding, Suzanne, and Del Balso, Anthony. *The Triple Crown Winners: The Story of America's Nine Superstar Race Horses*. New York: Parents Magazine Press, 1975.
Introduces the races that are part of the American Triple Crown and describes the breeding and training of the nine horses that have won this trophy.

FAU CLAIRE DISTRICT LIBRARY